Child Abuse

"Why Do My Parents Hit Me?"

by Kate Havelin

Consultant:
Martha Farrell Erickson, PhD
Director of Children, Youth, and Family Consortium
University of Minnesota

Perspectives on Relationships

Matters

pstone Press
), Minnesota

LifeMatters books are published by Capstone Press
818 North Willow Street • Mankato, Minnesota 56001
http://www.capstone-press.com

Printed in the United States of America

Library of Congress Cataloging-in-Publication Data
Havelin, Kate, 1961–
     Child abuse: why do my parents hit me? / Kate Havelin.
          p.   cm. — (Perspectives on relationships)
     Includes bibliographical references and index.
     Summary: Describes child abuse, its possible causes, its effects, and what can be done to stop it.
     ISBN 0-7368-0287-8 (book). — ISBN 0-7368-0295-9 (series)
     1. Child abuse—United States Juvenile literature. [1. Child abuse.] I. Title. II. Series.
     HV6626.52.H39 2000
     362.76—dc21   99-31165
                                            CIP

Staff Credits
Kristin Thoennes, Rebecca Aldridge, editors; Adam Lazar, designer; Heidi Schoof, photo researcher

Photo Credits
Cover: Index Stock Photography, Inc./©Myrleen Cate
Index Stock Photography, Inc./13, 21, 24; ©Myrleen Cate, 45
International Stock/©Michael Agliolo, 54; ©Elliott Smith, 27; ©Dusty Williams, 11; ©Scott Barrow, 59
Unicorn Stock Photos/©Dennis macDonald, 1, 7, 50, 53; ©Tom Edwards, 30; ©Jeff Greenberg, 40
Uniphoto Picture Agency/©Lew Lause, 8; ©Bob Daemmrich, 17; ©Rick Brady, 43
Visuals Unlimited/35; ©Jeff Greenberg, 58

A 0 9 8 7 6 5 4 3 2 1

Table of Contents

Chapter Overview

Many thousands of children are abused and neglected in North America every year.

The majority of abusers are the child's own parents.

There are four main types of abuse: physical abuse, emotional abuse, sexual abuse, and neglect. Neglect is the most common kind of child abuse.

Some experts believe emotional abuse can be the most damaging because it changes how a child feels about himself or herself.

Chapter 1

What Is Child Abuse?

The milk carton showed a picture of a smiling boy. The facts under the picture said **Sandy's Truth** the boy's name was Jacob. A stranger with a gun had abducted Jacob. Now Jacob's family and friends are trying to find him.

Sandy stared at Jacob's picture while she ate her breakfast. In school, Sandy learned to be careful about strangers. But no one warned her that parents also hurt kids. Sandy looked at the bruise on her arm where her dad had grabbed her. She felt the old scar where her mom's cigarette had burned her. Sandy looked at the picture of Jacob and began to cry.

Doctors and other professionals can get in legal trouble for not recognizing and reporting suspected child abuse.

The sad truth is that the people most likely to hurt children are their own parents. Almost three million American children are abused or neglected each year. Parents account for the majority of child abusers. Other abusers include stepparents, parents' live-in boyfriends or girlfriends, baby-sitters, neighbors, or even brothers and sisters. This book sometimes refers to parents as abusers. Most parents, however, do not abuse their children.

Types of Child Abuse

There are four main types of child abuse. Often children are hurt in more than one way.

Physical Abuse

Physical abuse includes any action that harms a person's body. Hitting, kicking, slapping, punching, burning, pulling hair, and poisoning are all examples of physical abuse. Shaking is the sort of physical abuse that is most dangerous to babies. An infant who has been shaken can be severely injured or even killed.

Sometimes physical injuries leave bruises, scars, or broken bones. Those marks often are signs of abuse. One doctor who saw many children with such signs named the problem. Dr. C. Henry Kempe came up with the name *battered child syndrome* in 1961. Dr. Kempe's phrase is still used. It describes a range of injuries children suffer due to abuse or neglect. In battered child syndrome, child abuse is defined as actions that cause injuries that doctors can diagnose.

Emotional Abuse

Emotional abuse includes anything that is said or done to hurt a
child's feelings or self-esteem. Frequently blaming a child for
something is one kind of emotional abuse. Frequently insulting a
child is another kind. Cruel words are not the only kind of abuse,
however. Some actions, like locking a child in a dark closet as
punishment, also are emotional abuse. Many experts say
emotional abuse is the most destructive abuse. This is because it
negatively affects how kids feel about themselves.

Neglect

Neglect means to ignore or choose not to take care of a child's
basic needs. Some parents neglect their children's physical needs.
They do not give their kids the right kind of food, clothing, or
place to live. Other parents neglect their children's emotional
needs. That means they do not treat their children with love or
kindness. They may pay little or no attention to their kids.

Some parents neglect their kids' educational needs. Those parents
make little or no effort to make sure their children attend school.
Neglect is the most common kind of child abuse. It happens more
than twice as often as physical abuse.

Bruce walks home from school slowly. **Bruce's Parents**
He knows there is no point in hurrying
home. His parents will not be there. The few times his parents
do come home, they are doing drugs or passed out. They pay
little attention to him. He wonders if his parents even
remember that he started junior high this year. All his parents
care about is cocaine and alcohol.

Bruce has learned to take care of himself, sort of. He sets his
alarm so he can get to school on time. He makes his own
meals—mostly cereal, sandwiches, and frozen food. When he
brings home papers from school that need a parent's signature,
Bruce signs them himself.

Bruce cannot remember the last time his parents hugged him.
He doesn't know when they got hooked on drugs. It seems like
it's been going on forever. They stopped cooking meals and
cleaning the apartment. They even stopped caring about Bruce.
Sometimes he thinks he should tell someone. But he is afraid
he will lose his parents. Bruce does not want them to go to jail.
He just wants them to stop doing drugs and start acting like
parents again.

Physical neglect accounts for 52 percent of all child abuse cases in the United States. Physical abuse accounts for 24 percent of all cases. Sexual abuse adds another 12 percent. Emotional and medical neglect together make up the rest of all child abuse cases.

Sexual Abuse

Sexual abuse is any action related to sex that harms a child. Sometimes adults force children to have sex. Incest is sexual abuse between a child and someone related to that child by birth or marriage. Other times, children are photographed or filmed having sex. Many experts think that sexual abuse is the most under-reported kind of child abuse. This book does not cover child sexual abuse. For more information and resources about sexual abuse, check the back of this book.

Is Spanking Abuse?

Studies show that many parents hit their young children. A mom may slap her two-year-old's hand for grabbing too many cookies. A dad may hit his son's bottom to teach him not to run out in the street. Many parents believe corporal punishment helps kids learn how to behave. Corporal punishment means using physical force to cause pain and teach a lesson.

A child is abused or neglected in the United States every 47 seconds.

Experts disagree about whether corporal punishment is good. One of the leading researchers on family violence believes spanking and other kinds of corporal punishment are bad. Murray Straus has studied thousands of families. Straus argues that spanking should be outlawed in America.

Straus believes spanking links love to violence. It teaches kids that it is okay to hit the people they love. Straus also says that kids who are spanked are more likely to be arrested or to assault another person. Many experts, however, do not consider spanking a form of child abuse unless it is hard enough to leave a mark. This book's definition of child abuse does not include corporal punishment.

How Many Children Are Abused?

The number of abused and neglected children has grown dramatically over the past several decades. This may be because more people are reporting it. Almost one million children were abused or neglected in 1996. That is an 18 percent increase in child abuse and neglect from 1990 through 1996. Since the mid-1990s, the level of abuse has seemed to remain stable.

Points to Consider

Why do you think so many children are abused?

What signs or symptoms might doctors look for in battered child syndrome?

Do you think spanking is child abuse? Why or why not?

Movies, TV, and music sometimes glorify violence. Do you see a connection between media violence and violence in families? Explain.

Why do you think neglect is the most common form of child abuse?

Chapter Overview

There is no excuse for child abuse, but many factors can increase the risk of abuse happening.

Child abuse does not happen because of children. Instead, it happens because the parent or other abuser fails to control himself or herself.

People who are at risk of becoming abusers may have been abused themselves or become parents too young. They may have too little experience to understand how to be a parent. Perhaps they have too little money or resources to cope with the pressures of a family. Some have physical or mental problems that distract them from parenting.

Chapter 2

Why Do Parents Hurt Their Children?

Donna never intended to get pregnant at 17. She loved her baby, **Donna Hits Her Boys** whom she named James. But a year later, Donna was pregnant again. Now Donna is 20 and has two kids. She does not have a job. Instead, she depends on welfare. She and her sons live in a small apartment. Some days Donna plays with the kids and has fun. Other days she feels burdened with all she has to do.

One day, Donna snapped. She hit James when he scribbled on the wall. She hit him again and again. When the baby screamed, she picked him up and shook him. She just wanted to be free and not be responsible for these kids. It felt like too much for her.

Home is not a safe place for many thousands of children. Often the people who claim to love children beat, starve, burn, or ignore them. It is hard to explain why parents or other adults abuse children. There is no excuse for child abuse.

Reasons Abuse May Happen

There are many reasons why child abuse happens.

Many parents do not know how to parent.

It is not easy to be a parent. Many people who have a baby are not prepared for the responsibility. They do not know how to care for a child. They do not understand child development. They expect children to do things that kids are not able to do.

Unfortunately, some people become parents while they are still too young. They are children or teenagers who are not ready to care for others. Parents who are very young are more likely to abuse children than are older parents. About 30,000 American girls under age 14 become pregnant each year.

Mothers are responsible for **75 percent** of mistreatment of children. Fathers are responsible for **46 percent** of mistreatment of children. Sometimes both parents mistreat children.

The abuser grew up being abused.

Violence is a learned behavior. Children whose parents use violence often end up repeating that behavior. Parents who were abused as children are six times more likely to abuse their own kids. If they get counseling, however, they may not pass on their own hurt to their children.

Many children grow up seeing domestic abuse. Domestic abuse is violence that happens within a home, usually between adults. Adults who hit their spouses are likely to hit their children as well. Domestic abuse and child abuse often happen in the same household.

Kids need to see peaceful ways to solve problems. Some children never see parents calmly talking out problems. Those kids do not learn peaceful ways to resolve conflict. Consequently, those children are more likely to be violent as adults.

Did You Know?

Single moms account for 30 percent of all the births in the United States.

Poverty can lead to abuse.

Children who grow up in very poor families are more likely than other children to be abused. No one knows exactly why this is so. Poor parents often face incredible stress. They may not have jobs, or their jobs may not pay them enough to support a family.

Research has found that children in families with an income of less than $15,000 are:

16 times more likely to be physically abused

40 times more likely to be physically neglected

29 times more likely to be emotionally neglected

56 times more likely to be educationally neglected (they may not get to school)

22 times more likely to be seriously injured from abuse

The abuser lacks self-esteem.

Adults who hurt children often do not feel good about themselves. The adults feel weak or unimportant. They may feel they have little power in the world. They take out their frustration on children who are smaller and weaker than they are. People who feel good about themselves are better able to handle stress. People with a poor self-image are more likely to blame others for problems. Children, especially young ones, can be easy targets for parents who are frustrated.

Isolation increases family stress.

Many families live far from grandparents and other relatives. They may not know their neighbors. Maybe they have few friends or people they can turn to for help. Being isolated, or cut off from others, increases the chances of abuse. Families who isolate themselves are more likely to be abusive.

Some abusers refuse to allow their spouse or children to have contact with other people. That isolation can prevent victims from telling others about their family's violence. Children who grow up with violence may believe all parents hit children.

Alcohol and drugs are tied to abuse.

Researchers are still trying to understand the connection between child abuse and substance abuse. Some studies show that one in three cases of child abuse occurs when the abuser is drinking. Alcohol abuse is a serious problem. Nearly 14 million people in the United States have a drinking problem. Many of those people hurt or neglect their families. Alcohol and other drugs sometimes make people feel freer to act out. These drugs can reduce people's ability to think clearly.

Tom's Dad Drinks Too Much

Tom loves his dad. He looks forward to Saturdays when they play touch football with neighbors. But Tom hates Sunday mornings. His dad usually is hung over from drinking countless beers. Tom and his sisters try to avoid their father after he drinks.

But this morning, Tom got caught. He was trying to get dressed quietly, but he dropped his shoe. His dad got mad and started hitting him. Tom's mother tried to protect him. Then she got hit. Her nose and lip were bleeding. Both she and Tom were crying when Tom's dad stormed out.

Child Abuse

An estimated 30 percent of all child abusers are under the influence of drugs or alcohol when the abuse happens.

The abusers are physically or mentally ill.

Some abusers are unable to care for children because they themselves are sick. People who are very sick may become wrapped up in their own problems. They may forget about the needs of others, including their own children. Parents who are physically or mentally ill may not have the energy to be good parents. People who are ill may not think clearly. They may not realize that they are mistreating their children.

Other Common Traits of Abusive Families

You cannot look at a person and tell he or she is an abuser. Child abuse happens in families of all races, religions, and economic levels. But abusers share the following common patterns.

Women are more likely to abuse children than men are.

Researchers believe that is because women have more responsibilities in caring for children. Also, more mothers are single parents than fathers are. Children of single parents are 77 percent more likely to be harmed than children who live with two parents.

Women are responsible for about three-fourths of all neglect cases. Men are responsible for almost three-fourths of sexual abuse cases.

Abusive parents do not connect well with their kids.
Studies show that abusive parents talk to their children less often than other parents do. When these parents do talk to their kids, they often yell at them or make them feel bad. Abusers also touch their children less.

Abusive parents are more likely to be too strict or too loose.
Two parenting styles are associated with abusive families. One style is the authoritarian style. That means parents rely on extreme discipline. Children and teenagers who challenge a parent's control may face abuse.

Children who live with too little discipline also are more likely to be mistreated. Parents who overindulge their children may be trying to win their children's friendship. Those parents may be desperate for closeness, so they let their children have their own way too often. They depend on their children to be there for them. When children grow and begin looking outside the family for friendship, these overindulgent parents may become angry. Those parents may use force to try to keep their children close to them.

Points to Consider

Do you think being a parent would be hard? Why or why not?

What do you think it takes to be a good parent?

Why do you think being poor increases the risks of child abuse?

Do you have relatives, friends, or neighbors that you could turn to for help if you needed it? Why do you think having people to turn to makes a difference?

Chapter Overview

Any child can be abused, but some children are more at risk.

Very young children and babies are most likely to be abused or neglected.

Children who seem different from others in the family may be more likely to be abused. Those children may be born prematurely. They may be more sickly or disabled. They may simply look different from the rest of the family.

Both boys and girls can be victims of abuse or neglect. Girls are more likely to be sexually abused. Boys are more likely to be neglected.

Chapter 3

Who Is at Risk of Being Abused?

Jeron and Julia are four-year-old twins. They usually play together pretty well. Of course, sometimes they fight. But their fights are nothing like the battles their parents have. Ever since the twins' new little brother was born, the household has been very tense.

Shaking the Baby

Baby Luis cries a lot. The parents do not get much sleep. Last night, Luis was up most of the night. The twins slept fine, but today their mother is exhausted. Julia grabs Jeron's toy truck, and he starts crying. Their mom starts yelling. Then Luis begins screaming. The next thing the twins see is their mom shaking Luis, shouting at him to be quiet.

Any child can be abused. Children need to know they are not responsible for the abuse. They are not to blame. Parents and other adults hurt children for their own reasons. Child abuse does not happen because a child did something wrong.

Risk Factors for Abuse

Some children face greater risks of being abused than other children. Six common risk factors children have for abuse are age, disability, appearance, unplanned pregnancy, family size, and gender.

Age

The younger a child is, the more likely he or she is to be abused. Children under one year old are most at risk. That is because babies are small and cannot do anything to protect themselves. Babies who are shaken can be seriously injured or die. The name for that is *shaken baby syndrome.* Babies who are not fed enough do not grow and thrive.

Children ages eight and older are more likely to be physically, sexually, or emotionally abused than younger kids. Younger children are more likely to be neglected, especially in terms of their medical needs, than older kids are.

Children who are older can defend themselves better. Some try to avoid their abuser. Some try to fight back. Some run away. But older children and teenagers still can be abused. Some experts believe the rate of abuse and neglect for teens is just as high for younger children. Teenagers, however, are less likely to report the abuse. Some teens may feel guilty. They may blame themselves for the injuries because they fought with their parents.

Some teenagers may decide that living on the street is safer than living with an abuser. Running away may get them away from an abuser, but homeless teens often face many other dangers in the streets.

Did You Know?

More than a million teenagers run away from home each year in the United States. Most of them stay within five miles of their home. And 85 percent of those runaways eventually reunite with their families.

Gender

Boys and girls each can be abused or neglected. However, boys and girls usually are hurt in different ways. More boys than girls are neglected, while more girls than boys are sexually abused. Girls are three times more likely to be sexually abused than boys. Because boys are not as likely to tell anyone about abuse, that number may not be accurate. Boys are 18 percent more likely to be emotionally neglected than girls. Boys also are somewhat more at risk of being seriously injured from abuse.

Laurel Is Stuck in the Middle

Laurel's parents got divorced last year when she was 12. Now she lives with her mother and sees her dad every other weekend. At times, Laurel wishes she could divorce both her parents. Her mom often is angry. Sometimes Laurel thinks her mom hates her because she looks like her dad.

Both parents try to get information from Laurel about the other parent. She feels stuck in the middle. She does not want to say bad things about either parent. Lately, Laurel's mom has been acting weird. She drinks too much and starts yelling and screaming. One night, she even started hitting Laurel with a hanger, screaming she wished Laurel had never been born.

Laurel is scared. She is afraid her mother will lose control and hit her again. She does not want to hear the angry things her mother says. But Laurel thinks if she tells her father, he will go to court and she will never get to see her mother. She doesn't know what to do.

Signs of Child Abuse

Child abuse often is hidden. Kids are afraid to tell others that they are being hurt. Sometimes children are killed before anyone outside the family learns about the abuse. Many people who work with children are trained to spot signs of abuse. Abused children may:

Seem very afraid of their parents or other adults

Often have bruises, cuts, or sores

Wear long sleeves and long pants during the summer to hide bruises

Have injuries that are not being treated

Cry too much or too little

Be too aggressive or too passive

Be afraid of physical contact, especially with adults

Be given inappropriate food, clothing, or medical care

Arrive at school too early and stay too late

Frequently fall asleep in class

Have undiagnosed learning problems

Fifty-three percent of child abuse victims in the United States are white. Twenty-seven percent are black. Eleven percent are Hispanic/Latino. American Indians, Asian Americans, and others make up the remaining **9** percent.

Points to Consider

Why do you think younger children are more likely to be abused than older children?

Why are kids in large families more likely to be neglected than kids in small families?

Do you think children who do not have siblings face more pressure than kids with siblings? Why or why not?

Why would kids who are abused be more likely to fall asleep in class than other kids?

Do you think running away is a good way to avoid child abuse? Why or why not? What could happen to a homeless child on the streets?

Chapter Overview

Children have been abused throughout history. Many societies believed children needed to be treated strictly so they would not grow up spoiled.

The story of one abused girl named Mary Ellen Wilson started the children's rights movement.

No laws protected Mary Ellen or other abused children more than 100 years ago in America.

The Society for the Prevention of Cruelty to Animals stepped in to help rescue Mary Ellen.

Many organizations now exist to protect and defend children's rights.

Chapter 4

A Look Back at One Child's Story

People have hurt or mistreated children throughout history. Ancient Greeks, Romans, Egyptians, and Aztecs all killed children in order to please the gods. Many countries considered children the property of parents or other adults. Many adults believed that children needed to be physically punished to grow up well.

The Pilgrims carried that stern attitude to America. New England passed the Body of Liberties law in 1641. That law said that youths over age 16 could be put to death for cursing or hitting their parents. Children simply did not have any legal rights. Still, adults who killed children could be punished.

Did You Know?

Factories used to employ children as young as age 5 to work 16-hour days. Sometimes the children would be chained with iron cuffs around their ankles to their machines. A law passed in 1802 forbid factories from taking orphaned or abandoned children. However, the law did not protect children whose parents sent them to work in the factories.

The earliest trial for child abuse happened in 1639 in Salem, Massachusetts. A man named Marmaduke Perry was charged with killing his young apprentice. The evidence showed that Perry had mistreated the boy, but it did not prove that he had caused the boy's fatal skull fracture. Perry was found not guilty.

The Case of Mary Ellen Wilson

The most famous case of child abuse happened to a 10-year-old girl named Mary Ellen Wilson. She lived in New York City in the 1870s. Mary Ellen's father died in the Civil War. Her mother did not have enough money to support Mary Ellen and was forced to give her up.

Mary Ellen went to an orphanage and was adopted by Thomas and Mary McCormick. When Thomas died, Mary McCormick married Francis Connelly. Her adoptive parents treated Mary Ellen cruelly. She seldom was fed and often was beaten with a "brutal whip of twisted leather."

A social worker named Etta Wheeler learned of Mary Ellen's frequent abuse. Wheeler wanted to help the little girl, but there were no local, state, or federal laws to protect children. So Wheeler turned to the Society for the Prevention of Cruelty to Animals (SPCA). She asked them to help rescue Mary Ellen. The SPCA went to court. They argued that because Mary Ellen was a member of the animal kingdom, she deserved safe treatment.

Mary Ellen's Trial

At her trial, Mary Ellen told the judge, "I don't know how old I am. I have had no shoes or stockings on this winter . . . . I have no recollection of ever being kissed . . . ."

Mary Ellen testified that her mother beat her every day: "She used to whip me with a twisted whip, a rawhide." The little girl showed the marks of her adoptive mother's meanness. She had two bruises on her head and a cut on her forehead from her mother's scissors.

Mary Ellen also recalled being locked in a bedroom when her mother left. The child told the judge she never remembered being outside her family's apartment: "I have no recollection of ever being in the street in my life," she said.

The number of abandoned or murdered babies grew drastically by the end of the Civil War. As a result, a group of nuns set up a hospital in 1869. The nuns set up cribs outside the hospital where parents would leave babies. Soon, the hospital was overwhelmed with abandoned babies. But other cities began setting up their own baby hospitals. The numbers of babies left to die began to shrink.

Judge Abraham R. Lawrence agreed that Mary Ellen needed to be protected. He ruled that the girl could be removed from her dangerous home. A jury later spent just 20 minutes to find Mary Ellen's adoptive mother guilty. Mary Connelly was sentenced to one year of hard labor. Mary Ellen was turned over to the Department of Charities and Corrections. The little girl was sent to a reformatory where she lived with teenage girls who had committed crimes.

Mary Ellen's New Home

Etta Wheeler again came to Mary Ellen's aid. Wheeler asked the judge to give Mary Ellen to her. The judge agreed, and Mary Ellen went to live with Wheeler's sister in upstate New York. There, Mary Ellen finally was allowed to have a safe and happy childhood. As Wheeler described it, "They taught her to play, to be unafraid, to know her rights, and to claim them. She shared her happy, busy life from the making of mud pies to charming birthday parties and was fast becoming a normal child."

Most early court cases of child abuse involved masters against servants or apprentices. Courts assumed parents had the right to do anything to their own children. Two of the only recorded court cases against colonial parents involved parents who refused to send their children to work or church.

Mary Ellen's story sparked adults to help protect other children. New Yorkers founded the Society for the Prevention of Cruelty to Children in 1874. Other states also began organizing groups to protect children. By the 1920s, more than 350 such groups were founded to safeguard children's rights.

Points to Consider

Why do you think children had so few rights throughout history?

Do you think children have rights equal to adults today? Explain.

Do you think Etta Wheeler was right to use an animal group, the SPCA, to save Mary Ellen? Why or why not?

What effect did the Civil War play in Mary Ellen's life? How do you think that current wars around the world shape the life of children?

Do you think other children were being mistreated like Mary Ellen was during the mid 1800s? Why or why not?

Chapter Overview

Child abuse does not stop on its own. Someone needs to intervene, or do something, to stop the abuse.

Telling someone often is the first step in stopping abuse.

Teachers, doctors, and many other professionals must report any suspected cases of child abuse.

Child protection workers must investigate all child abuse cases.

Courts can order families to get help and even can take away parents' rights. Sometimes courts and social workers do not do enough to protect children.

Chapter 5

What Happens When You Tell?

"Darcy, what's wrong? I wish you would talk to me and let me know why you are so sad."

Darcy's Secret

Grace knew her best friend Darcy was upset. But she did not know why Darcy had become so moody. Darcy had started crying as the two girls walked home from school. Darcy looked at her friend and sobbed, "You would never understand."

Do Not Keep Child Abuse Secret

The most important thing to do if you or a friend is being abused is to tell someone. Seek out an adult you can trust. Maybe you can tell a teacher, coach, neighbor, or relative. Many adults who work with children are required to report suspected child abuse. You can find someone to help you. Telling someone could save your life.

Telling someone about abuse can be hard. It is very important, however, that you make the effort to tell people about the abuse. It is dangerous to keep child abuse a secret. A friend may tell you he is being abused and ask you to keep his secret. You will help your friend more by telling his secret, even if you swore to secrecy.

You might tell someone who does not believe you. Do not let that stop you from telling someone else. Child abuse seldom stops by itself. Abusers usually cannot stop abusing without help. Keep telling others about the abuse until someone listens and helps. People will help you. Do not be afraid or embarrassed to report abuse. You will not be blamed. You will be helped.

Fifty-two percent of all child abuse reports come from professionals. Eighteen percent of all reports come from victims or their families. Nine percent of all reports come from friends or neighbors. The remaining 21 percent of child abuse reports come from others or are made anonymously.

Several hotlines are open 24 hours a day to help abused children. You can call any of the phone numbers listed below for help. Numbers that begin with 1-800 do not cost any money. The trained people who answer hotlines can refer you to someone in your area who can help. You also can look in a phone book under *Child Welfare, Child Protection Services,* or *Social Services.* The back of this book lists more options as well.

Helpful Hotlines

Boys Town 1-800-448-3000	Boys and girls in the United States or Canada can call this hotline for help.
Childhelp USA 1-800-422-4453	This hotline is for children and teens in the United States.
Kids Help Phone 1-800-668-6868	This hotline is for children and teens in Canada.
Covenant House Nineline 1-800-999-9999	This U.S. hotline is geared for runaways or kids who are thinking of running away.

Did You Know?

There were no effective laws requiring adults to report child abuse before 1964. But by 1968, all U.S. states had laws that called for professionals to report abuse.

Teachers and Doctors Must Report Abuse

The law requires many professionals such as teachers, doctors, nurses, police, and social workers to report suspected child abuse. That means they must tell Child Protection Services about any child they think is in danger. Some states also require many other professionals to report suspected abuse.

Child Protection Workers Check All Cases

Every state has child protection workers who investigate cases of suspected abuse. Social workers usually go to the place where the abuse happend. They talk with the children who reportedly were abused. They also talk to the suspected abusers. Sometimes they interview neighbors, teachers, or others who know the family.

The child protection workers may examine a child for signs of abuse or neglect. They may take a child to a hospital for doctors to check. Social workers can get court orders to remove children from danger. Sometimes that means social workers take children from their homes. Sometimes police arrest the suspected child abuser. This can be scary for kids, but it is the right thing to do. It often is the only way abusers get the help they need.

Child protection workers can ask families to agree to counseling or other services. Or the child protection agency can go to court to force a family to face its abuse. A judge may allow children to stay with abusive parents whom child protection workers will supervise. Some abused or neglected children are sent to a foster home while their family gets help.

Twenty-five percent of kids in foster care remain there for more than four years. Ten percent of those kids stay in foster care for more than seven years.

Foster Homes Can Help

Foster homes are places where children are supposed to be protected from abuse. Some foster homes are homes where families are trained to help children in need. Other foster homes are group homes or institutions with paid staff who supervise children. Some children stay in foster care for just a few days or weeks. On average, however, most kids remain in foster care for almost a year and a half.

Unfortunately, some foster parents abuse the children they are supposed to protect. This is rare, but it does happen.

Telling Someone May Not Fix Everything

Child protection workers cannot magically heal all of a family's problems. Life will not return to normal just because child protection workers are on the case. Many child abusers deny that they are hurting a child.

Unfortunately, some social service programs have too many cases and too little money to function well. That means it may take awhile before a child protection worker gets to a case. The child protection worker probably has many other reports to follow. Sometimes children continue to be hurt while social workers investigate their cases.

Some parents who are getting help may continue to hurt their children. It often takes a long time to teach abusers how to be better parents. Treatment and counseling may reduce an abuser's anger or drug problems. Treatment and counseling cannot, however, guarantee that a child will be safe.

The law gives parents 18 months to change their behavior and get their children back. Some children's advocates believe the government gives abusive parents too many chances to get children back. There is no limit to how many times children can be returned to homes in which they have been abused.

Sometimes a judge can terminate parental rights. That means the judge permanently separates children from their parents. Cutting all ties between parent and child is a last resort. Courts and child protection workers try to save families. They do everything they can to help parents learn how to care for their children better.

No One Protected Lisa Steinberg

One horrible story of child abuse happened in New York City in the 1980s. A lawyer named Joel Steinberg was supposed to find a good home for his client's newborn. Instead, Steinberg took the baby girl, named Lisa, to his own home. He and his live-in girlfriend, Hedda Nussbaum, had Lisa for six years. During that time, police often were called to the family's upper middle-class town house.

Neighbors often called police to report screams and cries coming from the couple's home. Police knew Steinberg repeatedly battered his girlfriend. But Nussbaum refused to press charges against her abusive boyfriend. No one thought to remove little Lisa or 16-month-old Mitchell from the home.

Police finally tried to rescue Lisa, but it was too late. She died at age six after being repeatedly battered. Her story shocked the country, partly because many people mistakenly thought child abuse did not happen in families with money.

Lisa's story is sad proof that abuse can happen anywhere and that sometimes authorities do not step in soon enough to save the victims.

Child protection workers checked out more than two million reports of child abuse in 1996. Those cases involved more than three million children.

Points to Consider

Who would you tell if you were being abused? Can you think of a friend, teacher, or relative who could help? Check your local phone book and find at least three places you could call for help.

Why do you think teachers are required to report child abuse?

What would you say if a friend told you he or she was being abused?

Why might courts give parents so many opportunities to keep their children?

Chapter Overview

Children have the right to be taken care of, the right not to be abused, and the right to go to court to stop their abuse or neglect.

Laws give children some special privileges that adults do not have. Children who go to court usually have the right to privacy so their name is not revealed.

Children have the right to sue. Some children have gone to court to divorce themselves from their parents.

Young people can go to court to become emancipated, meaning they are considered as independent as adults.

Chapter 6

Know Your Rights

Children today have many laws to protect them from abuse. Child abuse and neglect are against the law in every state and province. In the United States, people who abuse or neglect children are guilty of criminal and civil crimes. Criminal punishments include being fined or sent to jail. Civil punishments may involve taking parenting classes or getting drug treatment.

Children do not have all the same rights as adults. For example, children do not have the right to keep money that they earn. Young people also do not have the right to sign a lease or make a will. Still, children do have many of the same rights as adults. For example, young people who are arrested have a right to a lawyer.

The law does give young people some extra protections that adults do not get. Children who have been abused sometimes can give their testimony on videotape. That saves the child the pain and stress of testifying in court in front of the alleged abuser. Another extra protection children receive in court is a guardian ad litem. That's the formal title for a person that a judge appoints. The guardian watches out for a child's best interests in court.

Children Deserve Privacy

Perhaps the biggest protection that children receive in court is privacy. Child protective services are required to protect children's privacy. That means the name of abused or neglected children is not made public, even if the case goes to court. The main exception to the privacy rule concerns cases in which a child has died.

Some children's advocates say that privacy rules protect workers who do not do a good job. Advocates point to cases like that of Eliza Izquirdo, who died at age six after years of abuse by her mom and stepfather. Neighbors say they repeatedly told child protection workers about the abuse. Since Eliza died, lawmakers passed Eliza's Law. That law orders child protection offices to keep a child's abuse records for 10 years after the child turns 18. Eliza's Law also lets officials ask about previous reports of abuse, even if those reports were not proved.

Patty Goes to Court

Patty sat quietly in the courtroom with her lawyer on one side and her guardian on the other. She was going to tell the judge how her parents abused her. Her parents sat on the other side of the room with their lawyers. Patty did not want to look at them.

The judge smiled at Patty. Patty's lawyer told the judge a little about Patty's story. He told how she had been beaten and left alone for days at a time. The lawyer told how Patty's teacher noticed her bruises and reported the case. A child protection worker went to Patty's house and talked with her. Soon, Patty told the whole story. But Patty's parents swore they had never hit her. They said she was clumsy and had fallen and bruised herself. Patty knew they were lying.

Patty's guardian told her that many abusers lie about their violence. Still, it hurt to know her parents would lie about her. Today, Patty and her parents would each tell his or her side of the story.

Patty did not want to get her parents in trouble. But she did not want to go back to them. She liked the foster home she was in. She felt safe. When it was her turn, Patty went up to the witness stand and told her story. It was scary to be in court. Patty was glad to know that so many people were trying to help her. The judge, her lawyer, and her guardian would do what they could to protect her from more pain. That made Patty feel better.

The National Education Association has a Children's Bill of Rights. The teachers' group believes that every American child deserves:
- Proper food
- Medical care
- A safe place to live
- Freedom from abuse, violence, and discrimination

Many Child Abuse Laws Exist

The U.S. Congress has passed many laws to safeguard children. One important 1974 law was the Child Abuse Prevention and Treatment Act. That law created the National Center for Child Abuse and Neglect. The center coordinates the government's efforts to educate people about child abuse. The center has funded some 700 research projects to learn more about child abuse.

The federal government has passed many laws about child abuse, but states are responsible for enforcing those laws. States also have their own laws about abuse and neglect. For example, more than 20 states forbid teachers from spanking or using any kind of corporal punishment on students. Other states allow teachers to use some physical discipline.

Child abuse cases may end up in criminal or civil courts. Judges in those cases can decide what should happen to the abusers and victims. However, children can go to court for another reason. Children have the right to sue. That means they can ask a judge to fix a problem in their life. Several children have become famous because they had the courage to go to court.

Gregory was 12 years old **Gregory Divorced His Mother** when his story made the news. He went to court in Florida in 1992 to "divorce" himself from his mother, Rachel. She had put Gregory in foster care several times. Then she would disappear from his life for months or sometimes years. Eventually, Rachel always came back for Gregory.

Gregory was tired of bouncing from her home to foster homes. He had become part of one foster parents' family. He loved them and considered them his parents. Gregory did not want to go back to Rachel. He went to court and asked a judge to cut his legal ties to his mother.

Gregory won his case. The judge ruled that Rachel had abandoned and neglected Gregory. The boy, who made headlines around the country, got what he wanted. Gregory stayed with the foster family who loved him. They eventually adopted him.

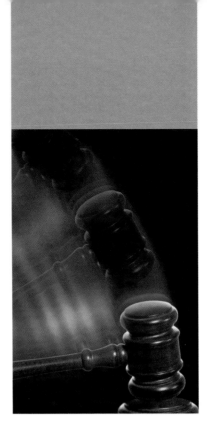

Emancipation

Some teenagers go to court to win their emancipation. That means they want the court to consider them an adult who is free to make decisions. Young people who are emancipated agree to be independent and support themselves. Their parents no longer are legally responsible for supporting them.

Young people under age 18 who marry or join the military are emancipated as well. Emancipation is one way for young people to break free from abusive parents. But there are many other ways children can get relief from abuse. Many organizations exist to help children who are being abused or neglected. Check the end of this book for more ideas on where to turn.

Parents have certain legal responsibilities toward their children. Parents need to provide their kids with food, clothing, shelter, and medical care. Stepparents who do not legally adopt their spouse's kids, however, are not required to support those children.

Points to Consider

Do you think courts and laws should treat children and adults exactly the same? Why or why not?

Why do you think children are given some special protections in court?

Do you know whether teachers in your state are allowed to use physical discipline? How could you find out?

Why do some teens go to court to become emancipated?

Chapter Overview

Children are not responsible for child abuse.

Child abuse and neglect are against the law.

Children who are abused or neglected need to tell someone.

The abuse can stop, and children can heal.

Chapter 7

Important Stuff to Remember

Children deserve to be treated with love and respect. People who hurt children must be stopped. You can help break the cycle of abuse. Here are some important points kids need to remember:

1. Children are not responsible for child abuse.

Child abuse happens because the abuser has a problem. The abuser needs to learn how to control his or her anger and emotions. Abuse does not happen because a child is bad. No child deserves to be hit. No child deserves to be neglected.

2. Child abuse and neglect are against the law.

Child abuse is wrong. Parents and other adults do not have the right to abuse or neglect children. Every state has laws against child abuse and neglect. Those laws can help protect children who are being abused or neglected.

3. Children who are abused or neglected need to tell someone.

Abusers seldom stop abusing on their own. Usually they need to get help before they can break the cycle of violence. Children who are being abused or neglected must tell someone. Many adults such as teachers, doctors, and social workers will report abuse. Reporting abuse or neglect to police or child protection is usually the first step toward solving the problem.

4. The abuse can stop, and children can heal.

Child protection workers and other professionals can protect children who are being hurt. They can separate abusers from their victims. Counselors can offer treatment and help victims and their families. That can help children feel good about themselves again. It is better for children to begin dealing with the pain of their abuse while they are still young. Abused and neglected children can heal.

Points to Consider

Who is responsible for abuse when it happens?

How can you learn more about laws on child abuse?

Why is it important to tell someone about abuse?

Glossary

abuse (uh-BYOOZ)—to treat a person or creature meanly

battered child syndrome (BAT-urd CHILDE SIN-drohm)—a medical term that describes a range of injuries to children that are caused by abuse or neglect

corporal punishment (KOR-por-uhl PUHN-ish-muhnt)—using physical force to cause pain in order to teach a lesson

crime (KRIME)—any action that is against the law

emancipation (i-man-si-PAY-shun)—the act of becoming free from a parent's control

foster home (FOSS-tur HOHM)—a place where a child can live away from his or her parents

guardian (GAR-dee-uhn)—an adult appointed by a judge to watch over a child's interests in court

guilt (GILT)—a feeling of shame about doing something wrong

incest (in-SEST)—sexual relations between two people who are so closely related that the law forbids them to marry

neglect (ni-GLEKT)—to ignore or choose not to take care of someone's basic needs

self-esteem (SELF ess-TEEM)—a feeling of pride and respect for yourself

shaken baby syndrome (SHAY-kin BAY-bee SIN-drohm)—a form of child abuse in which someone shakes a baby, causing injury or death

shame (SHAME)—a feeling of guilt or sadness

spanking (SPANG-king)—hitting someone with one's hand or an object, especially on the buttocks, to punish that person

violence (VYE-uh-luhnss)—words or actions that hurt people or things they care about

For More Information

Goldentyer, Debra. *Family Violence.* Austin, TX: Raintree Steck-Vaughn, 1995.

Havelin, Kate. *Family Violence: "My Parents Hurt Each Other!"* Mankato, MN: Capstone Press, 2000.

Havelin, Kate. *Incest: "Why Am I Afraid to Tell?"* Mankato, MN: Capstone Press, 2000.

Hyde, Margaret O. *Know About Abuse.* New York: Walker & Co., 1992.

Useful Addresses and Internet Sites

Institute for the Prevention of Child Abuse
25 Spadina Road
Toronto, ON M5R 2S9
CANADA

The National Clearinghouse on Child Abuse
and Neglect Information
330 C Street Southwest
Washington, DC 20447
1-800-FYI-3366

National Committee to Prevent Child Abuse
332 South Michigan Avenue
Suite 1600
Chicago, IL 60604

National Network for Youth
1319 F Street Northwest
Suite 401
Washington, DC 20004

Boys and Girls Clubs of America
http://www.bgca.org
Offers resources to help disadvantaged kids
from ages 6 to 18

Children's Defense Fund
http://www.childrensdefense.org
Provides education about the needs of children
so all children can have a safe and healthy start

The National Clearinghouse on Child Abuse
and Neglect Information
http://www.calib.com/nccanch
Offers information and resources about child
abuse

The National Exchange Club Foundation for
the Prevention of Child Abuse
http://www.preventchildabuse.com
Offers education and support to families
affected by child abuse

Index